MODAL VERBS

For Advanced, Business and IELTS English

Alexander Markham

TABLE OF CONTENTS

UNIT 1: WHY WE NEED MODAL VERBS IN ENGLISH

1.1 MODAL VERBS & ENGLISH

A modal verb is an auxiliary verb that expresses modality. That's to say, it indicates a state. That includes a level of possibility, need, obligation or advice.

Modal verbs are an integral part of the English Language and without a good understanding of how to use modal verbs correctly, it's not possible to read, write, speak or understand English at an advanced level or to pass advanced-level English examinations such as IELTS.

Modal verbs are extensively to modify main verb tenses to provide a wide range of different subtle meanings that are often unavailable without them in English.

1.2 WHAT IS A MODAL VERB?

Modal verbs are a subset of English auxiliary verbs. They are used to describe *modality*. This means they express *possibility, probability, ability, deduction, habits and hypothetical, imaginary and conditional situations.* They are commonly used to provide *politeness.* Most other languages do not have such a grammatically distinct class of modal auxiliary verbs which can make the concept of modals difficult to grasp for learners of English as a second language.

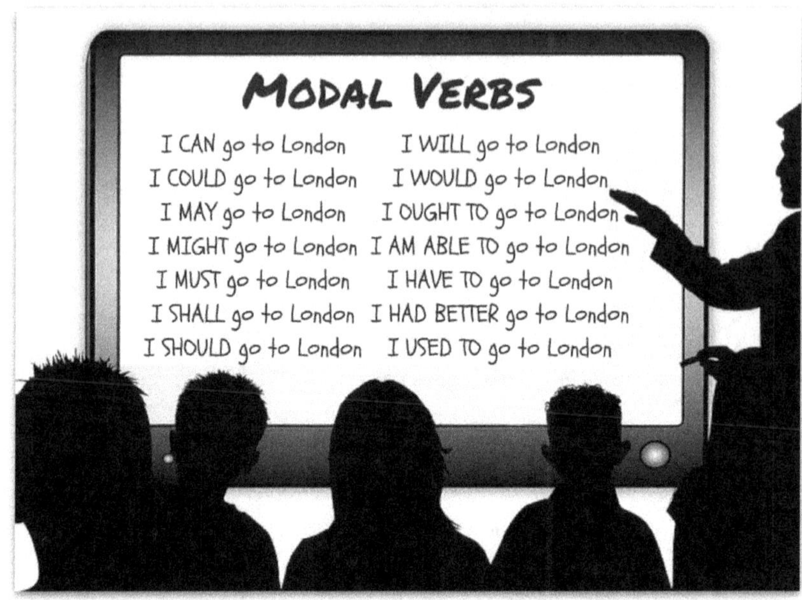

Each modal and semi-modal (see later units) verb modifies the main verb (go) differently.

This means that very sentence in the image has a slightly different meaning.

For example:

- *I CAN go to London* means I have the <u>ability</u> to go to London.
- *I MUST go to London* means I have the <u>obligation</u> to go to London and
- *I USED TO go* to London' means I <u>went</u> to London <u>many times in the past</u>.

1.3 ABOUT THIS BOOK

Throughout the book we look at not only the standard meanings but also at some non-standard everyday uses. Native speakers sometimes use modal verbs differently to what you find in standard English courses or grammar books.

As with any element of grammar in any language, the accepted standard rules of modal verbs may at times be ignored or used differently by many native speakers.

You will sometimes see a **NOTE** which provides additional or interesting information:

> **NOTE:** *A NOTE introduces additional information. This may be something important such information on how native speakers use modal verbs in everyday language.*

This book is aimed at intermediate and advanced-level learners of English as a Foreign Language and IELTS students, as a reference book for English tutors and for Business English students.

UNIT 2: HOW TO USE MODAL VERBS

2.1 WHAT DO MODAL VERBS DO?

English *modal verbs* are a set of *auxiliary* verbs used to express:

- *Possibility*
- *Probability*
- *Ability*
- *Deduction*
- *Habits*
- *Politeness* and
- *Hypothetical, imaginary and conditional situations.*

We use them to modify main verbs in order to express meanings that the main English verbs cannot provide on their own.

The English modal verbs, shown in their present and preterite (past tense) forms, are:

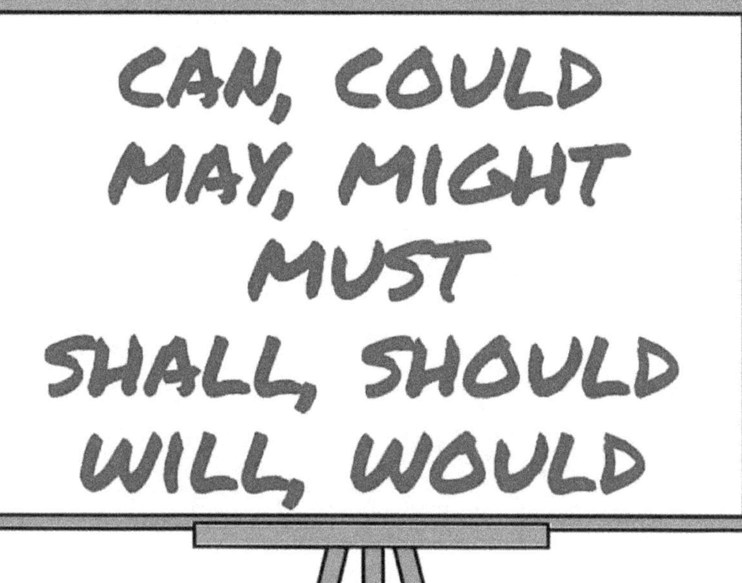

2.2 MODAL VERBS TENSES

All modal verbs have a present tense and a preterite (past) form, except for must which has a present tense only

For example:

> *Could* is the preterite form of *can, should is* the preterite form of *shall* and *would* the preterite tense of *will*.

2.3 PAST/PRETERITE

The preterite form in modal verbs is not, in most cases, used as a past tense.

Some modal verbs, such as *may* and *might* and *can and could,* have near identical meanings in many contexts. In other modal verbs, such as, *should* and *shall,* the meaning on the preterite is different entirely. *Shall* is a future strong assertion or plan whereas *should* indicates a recommendation.

For example:

- We *shall* got to the show – We are going to the show
- We *should* go to the show – We are expected to go to the show

The difference between standard and preterite modal form is often formality or conditionality rather than tense.

Could is the only modal preterite that is used as a true past simple tense of its present tense form, *can.*

2.4 THE CHARACTERISTICS

- Modal verbs function as *auxiliary verbs* and therefore *modify the main verb* in a sentence.

- A modal verb always appears *before* a main verb, unless it's a question.

- The main verb following a modal verb is always in the *bare-infinitive* form. The form is subject + modal verb + bare-infinitive. For example:

Subject +	Modal verb +	Bare-infinitive verb
You	can	speak
I	should	leave
He	must	wait

- Modal verbs are *defective.* That means they have no infinitive, participles, imperative, subjunctive or -ing forms. We have to use alternatives when we want to use any of these forms.

- Modal verbs do not *inflect.* This mean they don't take the -s ending in the third-person singular. For example:

  He *can* play piano **NOT** he ~~cans~~ play piano

- Modals have the same characteristics as the other auxiliary verbs, such as *have* and *do,* and undergo subject/verb inversion for questions:

  I can go now – *Can I go now?*
  You could help me – *Could you help me?*

- Modal verbs are *negated* by adding *not* after the modal verb and before the main verb:

  I *will not* go.
  You *must not* do that

  Can is negated by adding *not* to the modal verb to form one word; *cannot.*
  I *cannot* go to the match
  You *cannot* speak to me like that

NOTE: *The negative forms of modal verbs are usually contracted in spoken and informal English:*

Uncontracted negative	Contracted negative
cannot	can't
could not	couldn't
may not	never contracted
might not	mightn't
must not	mustn't
shall not	shan't
should not	shouldn't
will not	won't
would not	wouldn't

NOTE: *The contracted form of will not is won't. NOT* ~~win't~~

- Modal verbs cannot be used to modify other modal verbs.

  I *could* ~~*might*~~ go to the - I *could* go to the cinema

- Modal verbs can be used to modify other non-modal auxiliary verbs that have an infinitive:

  She ***must be*** over 80 years old

  I ***would have*** forgotten the time if you hadn't called

  You***'ll do*** better next time

NOTE: *Modal verbs are used without a main verb in tag questions and in replies to questions in informal English:*

- She can play guitar well, *can't she?*
- They would say that, *wouldn't they?*

- *Person A:* You should try harder. *Person B: Should I? Why?*
- *Person A:* You must leave now. *Person B: Must I?*

2.5 MULTIPLE MEANINGS

Modal verbs have more than one meaning or function. It is usually the context which makes clear which meaning is intended:

Example	Meaning
May I have some cake?	*Request / seeking permission*
I *may* try again later	Possibility
They *should* be arriving soon	*Logical deduction*
He *should* study harder	*Advice / recommendation*
He *can't* swim, he never learnt	*Ability*
He *can't* swim here, it's private	*Lack of permission*

More detail is given on multiple meaning in the unit on each individual modal verb.

2.6 AVOIDING DOUBLE MODALS

A modal verb cannot be used to modify another modal verb. We use a semi-modal or an appropriate adverb to replace the modal verb we want to modify.

- I ***might be able to*** do something about it, **NOT** I *might* ~~can~~ do something about it.
- I ***could possibly*** come tomorrow, **NOT** I *could* ~~might~~ come tomorrow.

UNIT 3: SEMI-MODAL VERBS

There are some other verbs and verb phrases that provide the same meanings as modal verbs. This means they also operate like auxiliary verbs and are used to express modality. They are referred to as semi-modals and are listed below:

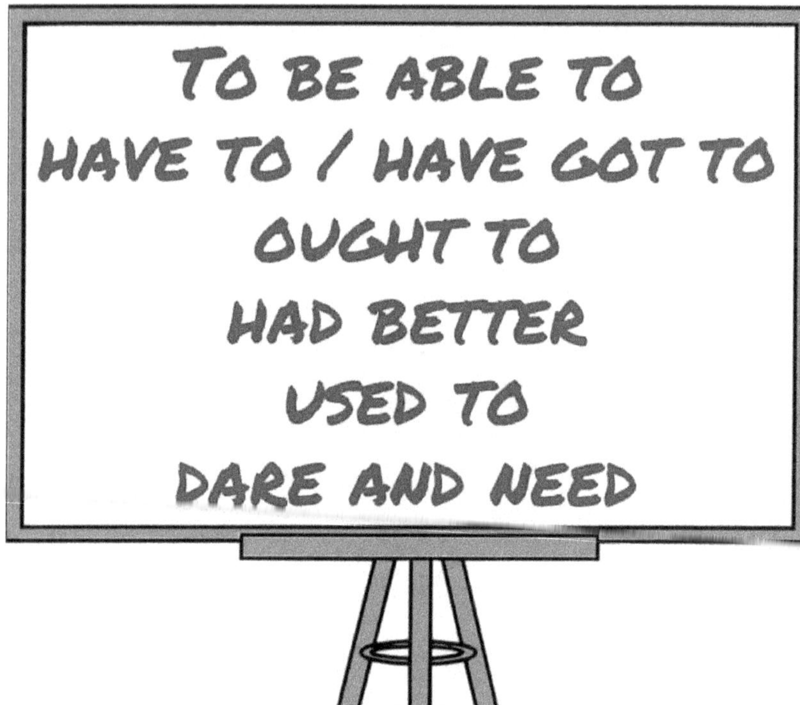

Although we use semi-modals to give the same type of modal meanings as modal verbs, semi-modals provide us with the ability to overcome some of the limitations of modal verbs. This means overcoming defective, the lack of past tenses and not being able to use double-modal verbs.

Ought to is often considered as a true modal verb in some English language books as it has identical characteristics to pure modal verbs, including being defective. However since it takes the *to-infinitive* rather than *bare-infinitive*, it is placed here with semi-modals.

Dare and *need* operate as modal verbs at times but more commonly, as main verbs.

UNIT 4: HOW TO USE THE PAST WITH MODALS

Although modal verbs are defective and have no past simple tense in most cases, there are various methods of referring to the past and still provide a modal meaning.

4.1 TRUE PAST WITH COULD

The only modal that can be used as a true past participle is *could* which is used in the past tense of *can* when referring to ability.

> He **could play** piano when he was young (*this is the past form of **he can play** piano*).

4.2 FUTURE IN THE PAST

All modal preterites can be used to describe the *future in the past* which is common in indirect speech.

> In the 1950s people **thought** that nuclear power **would** provide free electricity.

> I **told** him he **should** be careful

4.3 PAST HABITS

We use the preterite form *would* and the semi modal *used to* when talking about past habits.

Example	Meaning
I *would visit* my uncle every Saturday	*I regularly visited my uncle every Saturday*
I *used to visit* my uncle every Saturday	*I regularly visited my uncle every Saturday*

See the modal verb section on *will*, *would* and *used to* and the section on *habits* under modalities.

4.4 USING THE PAST TENSES OF SEMI-MODALS

We use the past tense version of a semi-modal to provide the past simple tense of a pure modal verb:

Present tense	Past tense
I *can play* guitar	I *was able to play* guitar
We *must work* harder	We *had to work* harder

Some modal verbs can be replaced by a main verb with a similar meaning when we want to speak about the past.

Present tense	Past tense
They *can win* the match	They *managed to win* the match
You *mustn't run*	You *weren't allowed to run*

4.5 MODAL VERB + PERFECT TENSE

In most cases, we use the modal verb with a perfect tense to give a past reference: *modal + have + past participle*.

Present form	Past form
You *should speak* to her	You *should have spoken* to her
He *may forget*	He *may have forgotten*
You *ought to speak* louder	You *ought to have spoken* louder

UNIT 5: HOW TO USE THE FUTURE WITH MODALS

Modal verbs in both their present and preterite forms can be used to refer to both the present or the future.

5.1 WILL, SHALL & SHOULD

The most common modal verbs used for the future are, *will* and *shall*. *Will* and *shall* have a near identical meaning but there are some important differences.

Should is also regularly used for the future despite being the preterite form of *shall*. The context of a sentence generally informs us what tense we mean.

English grammar books usually state the rule that *shall* is used for the 1st person (I and we) future and *will* is used for the 3rd person (you, he, she, it and they) future.

> **NOTE:** *Although many people do follow this grammar rule on shall and will, will and shall are also regularly used interchangeably by many native English speakers in everyday speech.*
>
> *Will is often used for 1st person future depending on the regional version of English being used. However, will and shall are both contracted to 'll, the difference is often irrelevant in spoken English and you shouldn't worry too much about the distinction when speaking with native speakers.*
>
> *Shall is in more common use in THE UK for the first person. It's also often used to provide more emphasis and certainty in constructions other than just 1st person. This is common in very formal or legal English.*
>
> *Listen out for these distinctions when speaking to a native speaker or if reading in English:*
>
> - *I **will** go shopping tomorrow. (A prediction)*
> - *I **shall** go shopping tomorrow (A promise)*

5.2 MODAL + BE + -ING

We also use modal verbs with the infinitive *be* and another verb in the *-ing* form to talk about future arrangements where there is some concept of continuous behaviour:

• *He **should be arriving** at 2pm tomorrow.*
• *They'**ll be taking** their exams next week.*

UNIT 6: MODAL MEANINGS WITHOUT MODALS

We can also express modal meanings such as *ability, obligation, permission* and *possibility* though a range of adjectives, nouns, adverbs and adverbial phrases:

Modal expression	Alternative using an adjective
He *may* be tired	It's *possible* he's tired
They *should* win the match	It's *probable* they'll win the match

Modal expression	Alternative using a noun
You *mustn't* worry	There's *no need* to worry
They *should* win the match	The *probability* is that they'll win the match

Modal expression	Alternative using an adverb
You *might not* like this	*Maybe* you won't like this
It *may* be a trick	*Perhaps* it's a trick

Modal expression	Alternative using an adverbial phrase
I *can* go to the show (permission not ability)	I *am allowed to* go to the theatre
I *could* go to the show (permission not ability)	I *was allowed to* go to the show
I *have to* do my home work tonight	I *am supposed to* do my homework tonight

NOTE: *Many learners, especially those whose first languages use different structures for modal meanings, tend to overuse adjectives, nouns, adverbs and adverbial phrases to express modal meanings.*

It is common for them to use adjective and adverbial expressions such as **it is <u>possible</u> that... or I have the <u>possibility</u> to... or it's <u>likely</u> that...**

Whilst this is grammatically correct, these structures are used less by native speakers in everyday language and can sound unusual if over used.

Compare:

> **"the probability is that they'll win"** *with* **"they should win."**

Although both essentially mean the same thing, the modal verb gives a more direct and straightforward meaning and is almost always the preferred choice for native speakers.

In reality, the alternatives to modal verbs often carry a subtle difference in meaning to the modal verb option.

Compare:

> **I have to do my home** with **I am supposed to do my homework.**

I have to do my homework expresses the obligation that someone has given to me do my homework and I don't have a choice. *I am supposed to do my homework* expresses the obligation that either me or someone else has given me. I may make the choice not to do it.

UNIT 7: THE MODAL AND SEMI-MODAL VERBS

7.1 CAN, COULD and TO BE ABLE TO

7.1.1 CAN

The modal verb *can* is one of the most commonly used modal verbs and expresses *ability* and *possibility*. It is also used for *requests* and *offers*.

- Questions with *can*

The *subject* and *can* are inverted to provide a question – *Can I help you?*

In the question form, *can* has two meanings: Do *I have the ability?* Or, for *a request or offer*. Therefore *can I help you?* means either:

- *Do I **have the ability to** help you?* Or,
- ***May** I help you? (a formal/polite offer)*

The context or the situation generally makes the intended meaning clear. If the situation is ambiguous it may be best to use another construction.

- Negatives with *can*

The negative form of *can* combines *can* and *not* into a single word; *cannot.*

This is the only negative modal verb that forms a single word. All the other uncontracted modal negative forms keep the *modal* and *not* as two separate words.

The contracted negative form of *can* is *can't*. The negative form reverses the meaning of *can* so *possibility* becomes *lack of possibility* and *ability* becomes *inability*.

> **NOTE** *Can't* or *cannot* are often used in expressions to express disbelief or doubt in the possibility of something.

For example, the response to a statement of fact you don't believe to be true could be:

- *That **can't be** true (I doubt the possibility that this is true)*
- *I **can't believe** that. (I don't believe the possibility of that)*

This structure is less confrontational for native English speakers than stating *that isn't true, which sounds aggressive* or *I don't believe that,* which can be taken as an accusation that the person is lying.

When referring to something in the past, *can't + perfect tense* is used. For example:

- *It can't have happened.* This means you don't believe it happened in the past.

NOTE: *Can't + infinitive* is also commonly used to express astonishment that something you know to be true happened but was entirely unexpected.

- *I can't believe he passed the exam because he never studied (but he did pass)*

Examples of how we use *can* and *can't:*

Modal meaning	Example	Non-modal explanation
Ability	I **can** speak English	*I have the ability to speak English / I know how to speak English*
	You **can** get the train from Kings Cross	*You have the ability to get the train from Kings Cross*
Lack of ability	I **can't** speak German	*I don't have the ability to speak German / I don't know how to speak German*
Offer	**Can** I help you?	*I am offering to help you.*
	Can you do that for me?	*Are you able to do that for me?*
Request	**Can** you help me?	*Are you able to help me?*

	Can I have a tea please?	*Are you able to give me a tea please*
Permission	You **can** relax now	*You have my permission to relax*
	You **can** borrow my hammer	*You have my permission to borrow my hammer*
Lack of permission	You **can't** borrow my hammer	*You don't have permission to borrow my hammer*
Possibility	There **can** be strong winds in the north of England	*There is a possibility of strong winds in the north of England*
Lack of possibility	You **can't** still be hungry, you've just eaten	*It's not possible for you to still be hungry...*

*NOTE: Native speakers commonly use can with verbs of perception such as see, hear, watch, feel, smell etc., Rather than say I see a butterfly, for example, a native speaker will use the form: I **can** see a butterfly. This would be a statement of fact meaning I am seeing a butterfly at this moment.*

7.1.2 COULD

Could is the preterite (past) form of *can*. *Could* is the only modal preterite that is regularly used as a true *past simple tense*.

Could is also used as the *conditional* form of *can* to describe *possibility, make polite requests, express past ability* and *make polite suggestions.*

Could, and other preterite modal verbs, are used with the *perfect tense* to talk about past hypothetical situations, also known as conditional sentences. It expresses a past ability or possibility which didn't happen but could have if something else had happened.

For example:

> - *I **could** have told him if I'd gone there (but I didn't go so I was unable to tell him).*

- Questions with could

The subject and *could* are inverted to ask a question. *Could I borrow this?*

> **NOTE:** Although *can* and *could* are both used to make requests, the conditional and preterite aspect of *could* makes the request sound more polite. Native speakers may feel that a direct request using a *main verb* or using *can* sounds aggressive or rude.

- Negatives with could

The negative form, *could not*, reverses the meaning of *could* and expresses *inability, impossibility* and *lack of permission*.

The negative form is regularly contracted to *couldn't* in informal and spoken English.

Examples of how we use could and couldn't:

Modal meaning	Example	Non-modal explanation
Past ability	When I was young I **could** speak English	*In the past she spoke English*
	She **couldn't** speak French	*She didn't speak French in the past*
	She **could've learnt** French	*She had the opportunity to learn French but didn't.*
Polite requests	**Could I ask** a question please?	*I politely request to ask a question*
	Could I have the bill please?	*I politely request that I receive the bill*
Polite suggestions	We **could try** the new restaurant	*I politely suggest we try the new restaurant*
	You **could ask** the	*I politely suggest you ask the police*

	police	
Possibilities	We **could be** in trouble	There is a possibility we will be in trouble
	You **could** always **try** again tomorrow	You have the possibility to try again tomorrow

7.1.3 TO BE ABLE TO

The expression *'to be able to'* is a semi-modal. It operates like a modal in meaning but not in form. We use this expression to express *ability*.

Unlike pure modal verbs, *to be able to* has the full range of tense forms and we used it to replace the defective true modal verbs *can* and *could* when expressing ability.

Tense	Form
Present	am/is able to
Past	was/were able to
Infinitive	to be able to
Subjunctive	be able to
Imperative	be able to
Continuous	being able to
Perfect	have been able to
Past perfect	had been able to

In the double modal mode, *to be able to* is used with all modal verbs except *can* and *could*.

For example:

- I *may be able to* come later   **NOT** I ~~could~~ be able to come later
- I *will be able to* repair this   **NOT** I ~~can~~ be able to repair this

- Questions with *to be able to*

The *subject* and *be* is inverted to form a question.

Examples of how to use questions with *to be able to.*

Example question	Meaning
Am I able to come in?	Do I have the ability or permission to come in?
Are you able to help me?	Can you help me?

- Negatives with to be able to

Not is inserted between be and able to form the negative; **to be not able to**. It expresses the opposite as the positive; an inability, for example: *I'm not able to play rugby.*

Examples of how we use *to be able to:*

Form	Example	Meaning
Can (pure modal)	I *am able to* speak English	*I can speak English*
	He*'s not able to* come to the phone.	*He can't come to the phone*
Could (pure modal)	She *was able to* speak French when she was young	*She could speak French when she was young*
Infinitive	I'd like **to be able to** travel to Argentina	*I would like to have the ability to travel to Argentina*
Subjunctive	I demand that he **be able to** leave	*I demand that he should be able to leave*
Continuous	I enjoy **being able to** watch TV every day	*I enjoy the ability to watch TV every day*
Perfect	I **have been able to** travel a lot	*I continue to travel a lot*
Past perfect	I **had been able to** travel a lot but I lost my job	*I used to travel a lot but I lost my job*

NOTE: *Although the imperative of to be able to exists grammatically and may be given in English grammar books, it is very rarely used in everyday English.*

NOTE: These days the subjunctive tense is becoming less widely used and is often replaced by the indicative or by the preterite modal verb *should* as shown in the table above.

So, the example *I demand he **be** able to leave* often becomes *I demand he **is** able to leave* or *I demand that he **should** be able to leave*. The construction with *should* is closer to the original subjunctive meaning.

7.2 MAY and MIGHT

7.2.1 MAY

The modal verb *may* is used to express *possibility, make formal or polite requests, show irrelevance, wishes or hopes* and for *giving formal permission.*

May is often used for formal situations and when extreme politeness is required.

When expressing possibility, *may* can also have future as well as present references.

May is used with the *perfect tense* to express *uncertainty* and *possibility* about a past event.

Example	Meaning
I *may have left* my phone in the café	*It's possible that I left my phone in the café*

May + perfect tense can never be used with permission or requests.

> **NOTE:** *May* (or *might*) with *be* is often used by native speakers to express that something is irrelevant despite the evidence of a contradicting fact. For example:
>
> - It *may (might) be* late but I'm not tired = *Despite the fact it's late, I'm not tired*
>
> - You *may (might) be* bigger than me but you don't scare me = *Although you're bigger than me you don't scare me*

- Questions with may

The *subject* and *may* are inverted to form a question or request. *May* makes the request or question formal and very polite.

Example	Meaning
May I come in please?	*I politely request to come in*
May I ask why this is broken?	*I politely ask why this is broken*

- Negatives with may

The negative form is *may not*; this is never contracted (~~mayn't~~). The negative is used for refusing permission formally or politely:

Example	Meaning
You **may not** do that	*Politely, you are not permitted to do that*

The negative form can also describe a possibility that something isn't as it seems:

Example	Meaning
That **may not** be correct	*It's possible that's not correct*

Some examples of how to use may:

Modal meaning	Example	Explanation
Possibility	*It may be broken*	*It's possible it's broken*
	It may not be broken	*It's possible it's not broken*
	I may have broken the TV	*It's possible I broke the TV (possibility about a past event)*
	We may go on holiday soon	*It's possible we'll go on holiday (future event)*
Polite permission	*You may leave now*	*You have permission to leave now*
	You may not wear shorts in the office	*You are not permitted/allowed to wear shorts in the office.*
Polite request	*May I borrow your mobile phone?*	*I politely request to borrow your mobile phone.*
	May I help you?	
Wishes and hopes	*May you live long and prosper*	*I hope that you live long and proper*

- Alternative forms for may

When *may* is used to express *permission* it can be replaced by *allowed to* or *permitted to* when you need to use a past or future tense.

For example:

Tense	Example	Meaning
Present	My father says I *may* stay up late	My father says I'm *allowed* to stay up late
Past	- - -	When I *was* young, my father *allowed* me to stay up late
Future	- - -	When I'm older, my father *will allow* me to stay up late

7.2.2 MIGHT

The preterite form *might* has a near identical meaning to *may* when expressing *possibilities*. *Might* is usually considered slightly less formal than *may* in this context.

Might can also express a slightly lesser degree of *possibility* than *may*. It can be used to talk about a *future possibility* in the same way as *may*.

While *might have* can have the meaning of *uncertainty* in the same way as *may have*, it can also refer to hypothetical possibilities in the past that did not occur but could have in other circumstances.

For example:

Example	Meaning
It *might have worked* if you'd tried harder	But the possibility of it working never happened because you didn't try harder (3rd conditional)

Unlike *may*, *might* is <u>**never**</u> used to give permission.

Might is <u>**never**</u> used for *hopes or wishes.*

I MIGHT go to London (IT'S POSSIBLE I will go to London)

- Questions with might

The subject and modal are inverted. *Might* is used for hesitant requests where you are unsure of the reaction of the listener.

For example:

- ***Might I*** ask if you're OK?

- Negatives with might

The negation of *might* is *might not.* It is sometimes contracted to *mightn't,* mainly in tag questions. It's not contracted as often as other modal negatives because *might not* can be easier to say than *mightn't* in some expressions.

Examples of how we use might:

Modal meaning	Example	Explanation
Possibility	It *might be* broken	*It's possible it's broken (lesser possibility than may)*
	It *might not be* broken	*It's possible it's not broken (lesser possibility than may)*
	I *might have broken* the TV	*It's possible I broke the TV (lesser possibility than may)*
	We *might go* on holiday soon	*It's possible we'll go on holiday soon (future) (lesser possibility than may)*
Hesitant request	*Might I borrow* your mobile phone?	*Is there a possibility you will allow me to borrow your mobile phone?*
	Might I help you?	*Is there a possibility you will allow me to help you?*

7.3 MUST, HAVE TO, HAVE GOT TO, HAD BETTER

7.3.1 MUST

Must expresses *obligation* and *necessity* from the point of view of the speaker or the writer.

It also expresses *necessity* when the object of the discussion is something persuasive or good. Finally it is used to express *a logical deduction.*

For example,

> • *It must be raining ahead as I can see dark clouds.*

When used for obligation, must refers to the obligation being imposed by the speaker.

Example	Meaning
We *must* leave now	*We are obliged to leave now*

Unlike the other modal verbs, *must* has no preterite form. When we are talking about *obligation* and *necessity* in the past, we use *had to* for these past obligations.

For example:

- Present: We **must** leave now
- Past: We **had to** leave

However, when the meaning of *must* is regarding *confident assumptions,* we can use the *past perfect* form after *must* (have + past participle).

For example:

Example	Meaning
I've lost my car keys. I **must've left** them in the café	*I'm confident I left my keys in the café*

- Questions with must

For questions, the subject and the modal are inverted. For example:

- **Must I** do that?

This means *do I have the obligation to do that?* or *is it necessary I do that?*

- Negatives with must

The negated form of *must* is *must not* which is usually contracted to *mustn't.* The negation applies to the *main verb*, not to *must*. Therefore, *you must not do this* means you are not permitted to do it.

When you want to express a *lack of obligation* or *necessity*, you should use *don't have to, don't need to* or *needn't.*

The negative form of *must* is not used when the meaning is *logical deduction*. Instead we use *can't* to express the confidence that something is not the case. For example:

- This **can't** be right <u>**NOT**</u> this ~~mustn't~~ be right - *This **mustn't** be right means there is a **probability** that something isn't right)*

Mustn't can be used as a simple negative of *must* in tag questions and some other questions expressing doubt.

- We ***must*** see you soon, ***mustn't we?***
- ***Mustn't he*** be in London by now? = He must be in London now

You MUST not smoke (You are NOT PERMITTED to smoke)

Examples of how we use must

Meaning	Example	Explanation
Obligation and necessity	You **must complete** this form	It's necessary you complete the form. (obligation set by the writer/speaker)
	You **mustn't make** any noise	It's necessary that you don't make any noise (obligation of the speaker)
	You **must see** this film	It's necessary to see the film (the implication being because it's good)
	I really **must lose** some weight	It's necessary to lose some weight (because it would be good for me)
Logical deduction	You **must be** the new employee	I believe with some certainty that you are the new employee
	I **must have left** my car keys at home	I'm fairly certain I left my car keys at home

- Alternatives for must

Since m*ust* is defective and has no past (preterite), perfect, continuous, infinitive or -ing form and cannot be used with other auxiliary verbs, *have to* is used for all obligations not in the present tense. The implication of the present tense obligation being the speaker's or someone else's is not used in the other tenses.

Example	Meaning
I **will have to** work hard (future)	*I will be obliged to work harder*
I **will ~~must~~** work harder	
I **had to** work harder (past)	*I was obliged to work harder (but now I'm not)*
I ~~**did must**~~ work harder	
I **have had to** work harder (perfect)	*I was obliged to work harder (and I am still working harder)*
I ~~have must~~ work harder	

7.3.2 HAVE TO and HAVE GOT TO

The semi-modal *have to* expresses *obligation and necessity.*

Have got to has an identical meaning to *have to* and is used as an alternative form in informal English in the present tense only. There is no difference in meaning between the two forms.

Have <u>got</u> to is not the present perfect tense of *have get,* it is a present tense. *Have got to* is almost always contracted to **'ve got to** in speech.

For example:

- I**'ve got to go** to work = I have a present obligation to go to work (because of an external reasons; I need to work to pay my bills or my employer insists or my husband/wife insists etc.)

In standard English grammar texts, *have (got) to* is defined as expressing *obligation* and *necessity* from the point of view of someone else, not the speaker or writer.

For example:

- You **have to** declare all your income in your tax return
- (The obligation is imposed by the government not the person explaining the obligation)
- Children **have to** use a child seat and seat belt when travelling in cars (the law obliges children to use a child seat and seat belt when travelling in a car).

Children have to use a child seat when travelling in cars (Because the law makes it a necessary obligation)

Have (got) to also provides other tense forms and moods of obligation and necessity for the defective modal *must*. The distinction between the obligation of the speaker *(must)* or someone else *(have to)* only exists in the present tense.

Have got to cannot be used in a past simple form. *Have to* only is used with the past simple even in informal speech.

For example:

Good example	Wrong example
We **had to** leave early	We **had got to** leave early
We **didn't have to** wait long	We **didn't have got to** wait long

| Why did you have to leave? | Why *did you have got to* leave? |

Have got to cannot be used when another modal verb occurs. You must use **have to**:

Good example	Wrong example
They **will have to** return the money	They **will have got to** return the money X

- Questions with have (got) to

Have to uses the auxiliary *do* to form questions.

For example:

- **Do I have to** queue here?

> **NOTE:** *Older text books and some literary forms of English occasionally use an inversion of have and the subject to form a question. This should be avoided in everyday language use as it sounds odd today.*

Have got to inverts the subject and *have to* form the question;

- **Have I got to** queue here?

- Negatives for have to and have got to

The negated form of *have to* uses the auxiliary verb *do + not: do not have to*. This is commonly contracted to <u>don't</u> have to.

The negated form of *have got to* is *have <u>not</u> got to*, which is informal and therefore usually contracted to *have<u>n't</u> got to* in speech.

How we use *have to* and *have got to:*

Meaning	Example	Explanation
Obligation or	I **have to** work	It's necessary that I work late due to

necessity	late tonight	*someone else's obligation on me.*
	I **had to** work late tonight	*I was obliged to work late tonight. (It may have been mine or someone else's obligation)*
	You **have to** taste this chicken	*It's necessary you taste this chicken (persuasion because it's so good)*
	You**'ve got to** taste this chicken	*Informal, it's necessary you taste this chicken (persuasion because it's so good)*
	Don't you have to work late tomorrow?	*Question form using auxiliary do + not.*
	Haven't you got to work late tomorrow	*Informal structure.*

NOTE: *Using must for the speaker's obligation and have (got) to for someone else's obligation is the standard grammatical explanation provided in English grammar books and courses. However, this is a general rule and may not be the case in all English speaking regions.*

Even in regions where this distinction applies, native speakers won't always make this grammatical distinction. Some people will use have to for all obligations and must for logical deductions.

7.3.3 HAD BETTER

Had better is similar in use to pure modal verbs except that it consists of two words. It follows all the other characteristics of pure modal verbs.

We use *had better* to give *advice* and *recommendations,* similar to *should* and *ought to.* It is usually contracted to *'d better* in informal and spoken English.

Although we use the past tense *had* rather than *have, had better* is used for present and future forms.

Had better is a stronger expression of advice and recommendation than *should* or *ought to.* We use it if we think there will be negative results if someone does not do what is desired or suggested.

Examples:

Example	Meaning
You **had better** check the car	*I advise you to check the car (otherwise there will be a problem)*
I'd better go now	*I ought to go now (otherwise I'll be late)*

- Questions with *had better*

The question form is formed by reversing the subject and had. This has a similar meaning as *should* and *ought to* when used for advice and recommendations but sounds more formal.

Example	Meaning
Had we better speak to them first?	*Should we speak to them first?*
Had I better look somewhere else?	*Should I look somewhere else?*

NOTE: Most native speakers avoid *had better* in question form preferring to use *should, ought to* or the negative form, *hadn't (subject) better*.

The negative form of had better is *had better not,* contracted to *'d better not.*

Example	Meaning
You***'d better not*** leave until it stops raining	*I advise/recommend you don't leave...*
Hadn't you better wear something warmer?	*Shouldn't you wear something warmer?*

7.4 NEED & DARE

Need and dare are unusual in that they can be used as both normal verbs and modal verbs. Both can also be nouns.

7.4.1 NEED

The modal use of *need* expresses *obligation* and *necessity* and is very similar in meaning to *must* and *have to.*

Need is a semi-modal verb as it is also used as a main verb (and as a noun). As a main verb it operates in the same way as all verbs with a full range of tenses and forms. As a modal verb, *need* follows the modal verb rules such as linking to a bare infinitive, no 3rd person 's' and no past tense.

Need has a slightly old fashioned or formal sound as a modal verb for many native speakers and is mostly used in negative and interrogative sentences and in sentences which express doubt or negative ideas.

Example	Meaning
Need I tell you that it's late?	*Do I have to tell you it's late?*
Need you do that?	*Must you do that? Do you have to do that?*

- **Questions with *need***

The subject and the semi-modal *need* change position to form questions, *need I remember this?* When used as a main verb, *need* uses the auxiliary verb do to form questions. The question form of *need* as a semi-modal verb is not very common as it's considered formal and old fashioned.

Example	Meaning
Need we wait here?	*Must we / do we have to wait here?*

Need she use a child seat? Yes she **has to** use a child seat.

- Negatives with *need*

The negated form of *need* is *need not* which is contracted to *needn't*. *Needn't* is used as the negative form of *must* when *must* means obligation or necessity and is very similar to the meaning of *didn't have to*. (*Must not* expresses prohibition).

Example	Meaning
You **needn't** worry, it'll be fine	*Do do not have to worry, it'll be fine*

NOTE: *English grammar text books and courses often teach that we use* **need** *and* **needn't** *to express the obligations of the speaker or writer in a similar way to must.*

7.4.2 DARE

Dare means to have courage or bravery to do something. *Dare* is a semi-modal since it is also used as a main verb and as a noun – a dare is a challenge.

As a main verb it operates like all verbs but as a modal verb, *dare* follows the modal verb rules such as linking to a bare-infinitive, having no 3rd person -s and having no past tense.

Dare is generally used for questions and negative sentences.

Examples	Meanings
She **dare not** speak	She doesn't have the courage to speak
Dare he tell them?	Is he brave enough to tell them?

<u>Dare</u> he enter the burning building? Does he <u>have the courage to</u> enter the burning building? Yes.

- *Would he dare to tell them?* (main verb) vs *She wouldn't dare tell them* (modal verb).

NOTE: *Dare as a modal verb is often employed in literature to give a feeling of drama.*

- *No one dare go to the woods.*

NOTE: Dare as a modal verb is used in several common idioms and expressions:

- **How dare you** (do that), **How dare she** (say that) – expressions of outrage.
- **I dare say** (or **I daresay**) – expression of believe in what the speaker is saying.
- **I dare say** – *an idiomatic expression used for saying that something is possibly true although you do not know for certain. Often used with irony or sarcasm.*

- Questions with dare

The subject and modal verb are inverted for questions:

- *Dare* he go there?
- *Dare* he do that?

These expressions mean *does he have the courage* to go or do something?

Where dare is used as a main verb then the auxiliary verb *do* is used to form a question and this is the most common usage:

Does he dare to go there?

- Negatives with dare

The negative form of *dare* is *dare not* which is also contracted to *daren't.*

The negative form *dare not* is the opposite of *dare* and means a *lack* of courage or bravery to do something.

Example	Meaning
I *dare not* interrupt	*I don't have the courage to interrupt*
He ***daren't*** go there	*He doesn't have the courage to go there*
No one dare go there	*No one has the courage to go there*

7.5 SHALL, SHOULD and OUGHT TO

7.5.1 SHALL

Shall is used to indicate future actions. It is an alternative to *will* in some situations although *will* is more commonly used.

Although s*hall* is similar to *will*, there are some differences. The traditional grammar rule is that modal verb *shall* is used to indicate the future action in the 1st person: *I shall and we shall*. Whereas the 2nd and 3rd person subject use *will* for the future.

Shall is contracted to ***'ll*** like will.

Shall is often used to give a stronger meaning than *will*.

Shall indicates a future action for *promises*, *certainty* and *inevitability*:

Examples	Meanings
I **shall** help you	*I promise to help you*
I **shall** never forget the day I arrived	*I am certain I will never forget the day I arrived*
One day, he **shall** be king	*It's inevitable that one day he will be king*

> **NOTE:** *In practice, native English speakers don't always differentiate between shall and will. Since the contraction, **'ll**, is identical for both, it's often irrelevant anyway.*

Shall can be used with the perfect tense (*shall have (done)*) in the 1st person to provide the future in the past. For example:

- By next Monday I ***shall have finished*** the painting.

The future _shall_ be ours

Shall can be used for the 2nd and 3rd person subjects when you want to indicate an order or a _prophecy_. This form is usually only used in very formal writing, such as legal documents, literature, specifications and regulations:

- _Any person causing a disturbance **shall** be reported to the police._
- _Those unable to pay their rent **shall** be evicted after six months_
- _Cinderella, you **shall** go to the ball._

- Questions with shall

The subject and modal verb are reversed for questions: _shall I start?_

Shall is commonly used in questions in the 1st person. It is used to make _polite suggestions or offers_ and _to ask for advice._

In the question form, _will_ has another meaning so is not interchangeable unless used with a question word such as what or why.

Example	Meaning
Shall we go now?	I politely suggest we go now
Shall I do this for you?	I offer to do this for you
What shall we do with this?	I'm asking for advice about what to do with this

- Negatives with shall

The negative form is *shall not* which can be contracted to *shan't.*

Shan't is used to express *strong future intentions.* It has a stronger intention than *will not.*

- *We **shan't** let you down*
- *We **shan't** forget*

7.5.2 SHOULD

Should is the preterite (past) form of *shall. Should* is never used as a true *past simple* tense.

Should is a very important modal verb and is used for a large number of meanings depending on the context:

- *Advice, suggestions or recommendations*
- *Possibility and probability*
- *A condition*
- *To make a statement more polite*
- *An expectation*

Should is regularly used in the following constructions using the meanings shown above.

With conjunctions '*in case*' and '*if*':

- We bought a blanket ***in case*** you ***should*** feel cold *(possibility)*
- ***If*** you feel cold you ***should*** put a warm coat on *(recommendation/advice)*

After adjectives of feeling such as: *anxious, concerned, disappointed, eager, excited, glad, happy, pleased:*

- I'm ***concerned*** that he ***should*** think that way *(a condition, he thinks that way)*
- They are ***anxious*** that you ***should*** refuse it *(possibility)*

Should is often used as a replacement for the *present subjunctive* after verbs **such as** *demand (that), insist (that), recommend (that), request (that), suggest (that).*

- She's *insisting (that)* he **should** leave now *(She's insisting (that) he **leave** now (present subjunctive) - recommendation)*

- *I **suggest (that)** he **should** ask for a delay* (I suggest that he **ask** for a delay (present subjunctive) – recommendation/advice)

- *We **recommend (that)** you **should** wait until later* (We recommend (that) you **wait** until later (subjunctive) - advice)

After noun expressions such as *the fact that* and *the idea that*:

- ***The fact that*** they don't like it doesn't mean we ***should*** stop *(recommendation)*

- We don't like ***the idea that*** we ***should*** stop going there.

With the perfect tense – *should have + past participle* – to express something that was expected in the past but didn't happen.

- *You **should have finished** that last week* (I expected you to have finished that last week but you didn't)

In conditional sentences:

- *We **should** think about finishing the plan **next week*** (recommendation)

- ***Should*** *you need anything please let me know* (replaces ***if*** in many conditional sentences – possibility)

- If we win, we ***should*** thank our fans

A prediction or expectation that something will happen using the structure:

Should + be + past participle

- We ***should be finished*** by 9pm – *(we expect/predict that we will be finished by 9am)*
- I **shouldn't be** too late. *(I don't expect to be late)*

Or, shouldn't + have to + verb

- We ***shouldn't have to*** wait too long – *(We don't expect to have to wait too long)*

The future <u>should</u> be a wonderful thing

- Questions with should

The subject and should are inverted to form *questions*. It is used to *ask advice* or to make a *polite suggestion* when you are not sure of a positive answer.

Example	Meaning
Should you call the doctor?	*Polite suggestion*
Should we stay or go	*Asking advice*

- Negatives with should

The negative is formed by *should not* which can be contracted to *shouldn't*. It's used to give *advice,* usually about something you think is wrong.

The negation is applied to the main verb and not the modal.

For example:

Example	Meaning
You **shouldn't** do that	*My advice I that it's wrong to do that*
You **shouldn't** show him that	*My advice is that it's wrong to show him*

picture	*that picture*

- Alternative forms

Should can be replaced by *be supposed to* when it means something that was intended to happen. This allows the forms *was/were supposed to,(to), be supposed to* and *being/been supposed to.*

Like other modal verbs, should can be used with the perfect tenses.

Modal	Non-modal
Should I have been at the meeting?	*Was I supposed to be at the meeting?*
Should she have been at the meeting?	*Was she supposed to be at the meeting*

7.5.3 OUGHT TO

Ought to is a semi-model verb that has identical characteristics to pure modal verbs with the exception that it uses the *to-infinitive.* For this reason of syntax, it's considered as a semi-modal. It has a near identical meaning to *should when used* for *advice, suggestion, intentions recommendations* and *probability.*

Generally, native speakers use either *ought to* or *should* based on personal preference and to avoid repetition.

Ought to can sometimes be considered to be more objective that *should* for some native speakers, that's to say they consider it removes the personal feeling from what they are saying.

This sometimes drives the decision between the two similar options:

Modality	Example using ought to	Example should
Recommendation / advice/ suggestion	You **ought to** take this back to the shop	*You **should** take this back to the shop*
	If you feel cold,	*If you feel cold, you **should** put a*

| you ***ought to*** put a warm coat on | *warm coat on* |

| **Expectation / prediction** | We ***ought to*** be finished by 9pm | *We **should** be finished by 9pm* |

You <u>ought to</u> spend less money (I <u>recommend</u> you spend less money)

- Questions with ought to

As with other modal verbs, the subject and ought are reversed to form the question. The to is usually dropped:

- ***Ought I*** do this?
- ***Ought I*** be doing this

In practice we tend to use should for non-negative questions and the negative form of *ought to* for questions. We leave out *to* in question tags but not in questions.

- We ***ought to*** pack our bags, ***oughtn't we?***

- Negatives with ought to

The negated form is *ought not* or *oughtn't*. This is equivalent in meaning to *shouldn't* which is generally preferred by native speakers:

- You *ought not to* do that

- *We ought to pack our bags, **oughtn't we?***

- *We ought to pack our bags, **ought we not?***

- Alternative forms

As with should, *ought to* can be replaced by *be supposed to* when it means *intention*. This allows the forms *was/were supposed to, be supposed to, being supposed to and been supposed to.*

7.6 WILL, WOULD and USED TO

7.6.1 WILL

Will is used as a modal verb and as an auxiliary verb to indicate future actions. It is often referred to as the future tense of English (together with shall).

We use *will* to talk about the future with *promises about future actions, predictions about the future, orders that indicate a future action* and *offers to complete a future action.*

For other future meanings such as arrangements, timetables and plans we use alternative ways of indicating the future in English such as *going to, the present simple + time* and *the continuous tense.*

As a future tense, *will* is used for the simple future (*e.g. will be*), future continuous (*e.g. will be doing*), future perfect (*e.g. will have done*) and the future perfect continuous (*e.g. will have been doing*).

Will can be used to express *annoying habitual actions.* The context, the lack of the contracted form and the stress and strong pronunciation of *will* all indicate the meaning. For example:

Example	Meaning
He **_will_** insist on talking too loudly	He's always talking too loudly and it's annoying (regular habit – will is stressed and uncontracted)
He'*ll* insist on talking too loudly	I predict he's going to speak too loudly (future action – will is unstressed and contracted)
They **_will_** always complain when they are in a restaurant	They always complain in a restaurant and it's annoying (regular habit – will is stressed and uncontracted)
They'*ll* complain when they are in the restaurant	I predict that they will complain in the restaurant (future action – will is uncontracted and unstressed)

*I **will** do that in the future*

- **Questions with will**

The subject and *will* are inverted to form a question:

- **Will you** wait for me?

- When **will she** send the package?

- **Negatives with will**

The negative form is **will not**. The contracted form is **won't** (NOT ~~willn't~~ X). In the modal meanings of *will*, the negation is effectively applied to the main verb and not to the modal *will*. For example:

- You will **not do it** = *I order you **not to do it**.*

- How to use will

Will for promises (about a future action)

Example	Meaning
I**'ll** call you tomorrow	*I promise to call you tomorrow*
He told me he**'ll** try harder	*He told me that he promises to try harder (in the future)*
I **won't** let you down	*I promise that I will not let you down*

Will for predictions (about a future action)

Example	Meaning
I believe they**'ll** win the game	*I predict that they will win (at the end of the game which is in the future)*
I don't think it **will** rain tomorrow	*I predict that it will not rain tomorrow*
I reckon that John **won't** be coming	*I predict that John is not coming*
I can hear the phone ringing, that **will** be my mum calling	*I can hear the phone ringing, I predict that's my mum calling*
By 2050, we **will have eliminated** world poverty	*A future prediction using the future in the past*

The two examples above, *John won't be coming* and *that will be my mum*, have an immediate future meaning, possibly just an instant in the future.

Will for orders (about a future action)

Example	Meaning
You **will** finish this project by 9pm	*I order you to finish the project by 9pm*
You **will** go to them and apologise	*I order you to go to them and apologise*

You **will _not leave_** until you've finished	_I order you <u>not to leave</u> until you've finished_

Will for offers and requests (about a future action)

Example	Meaning
I**'ll** help you to paint the house	_I offer to paint the house (as a future action_
Will you work for me?	_I'm asking if you will work for me?_

Will to express annoying habitual habits

Example	Meaning
He **_will_** make a noise when he eats	_He always makes a noise when he eats and it's annoying_

NOTE: _In spoken English stress is often used to differentiate between will to indicate an annoying habit and will to indicate the future. For more information see part 4, pronunciation and stresses with modal verbs._

7.6.2 WOULD

The preterite form would is used as the _past tense of will_ and as a _conditional form_. It can also be used as a past tense of _shall_ where the speaker uses _shall_ for 1st person future simple. It is also used to describe _past repeated actions._

Would is often contracted to **_'d_** in informal language and speech, as in: I**_'d_** like some coffee.

> **NOTE:** _'Would' and 'had' have the same contraction 'd. Identifying the correct uncontracted verb is straightforward – 'would' precedes a bare-infinitive and 'had' precedes a past tense (or a to-infinitive usually uncontracted)_
>
> _For example I'd finish (would) and I'd finished (had)._

- Would is used to express:

- _The conditional future_

- _The past_

- _Past habits and behaviours_

- _to talk about the past from a future perspective (future in the past),_

- *Hypothetical situations*

- *To introduce opinions*

- *To indicate willingness*

- *To state desires and wishes*

- *To make polite requests*

- *To indicate preferences*

- *To show possibility*

- *To indicate disapproval*

- *To give advice.*

- Would as a past tense

Would can be used not only as the *past tense* of *will* but also as *past perfect tense – I would have gone (but I didn't))* and the *future perfect* in conditionals – *I would have* a lot of money if I won the lottery.

Past tenses are also commonly used in English to provide remoteness. All uses of *would* provide remoteness, these may be remoteness between speakers which makes expressions more polite, remoteness in time (past tense) and remoteness of possibility.

- Would for polite requests

Would is commonly used to make polite requests. Typically it can replace *want* which can sound too direct for native English speakers. For example, saying *I want something* could be considered rude by native speakers who prefer to use *I would like something* which is a more friendly and polite request. Another example of using *would* for politeness is to say *would you do this?* instead of *(please) do this.*

NOTE: *The form for 'would' is the same as for all other modal verbs:*

Subject + modal verb + main verb.

However in informal and spoken English the main verb is often left out when the meaning is obvious to the listener.

For example:

John: *I'd like to help you.* Anne: *Would you?* (like to help me)

Jane: *Would you like to read this book?* Susan: *I would* (like to read the book)

I would love a cup of coffee

- Questions with would

The subject and would are inverted to form questions:

- **Would you** like an ice cream?

- Negatives with would

The negated form is *would not* which is contracted to *wouldn't*:

- I wish you **wouldn't** do that

- How to use would

Would as the past tense of will:

Example	Meaning
When I arrived he told me he **would help** me	*Present tense form: as I arrive he tells me he* **will help** *me*
I thought I **would be** late	*Present tense form: I think I'll **be** late*
They said they **would have to take** the train	*Present tense form: they say they **will have to take** the train*
They **would have been** home	*Future in the past. Present tense = The train is*

by now but the train was late   *on time and they **will be** home soon*

Would for past habits and behaviours:

Example	Meaning
When I was young I **would play** football everyday	*When I was young I **played** football / I **used to play** football everyday*
When I was young I **would visit** my grandmother at the weekend	*When I was young I **used to visit** my grandmother at the weekend*

NOTE: *When would is used to describe past habits or behaviours in the past, it is often meant with a feeling of nostalgia.*

NOTE: *Would cannot be used for a past habit when the main verb following it is a stative verb, that's to say a verb that describes a state rather than an action:*

- *When I was young I ~~would love~~ to visit my grandmother (love is a stative verb)*

When you want to use a stative verb for a past habit you need to use used to or a past simple;

When I was young I <u>loved</u> to visit my grandmother / When I was young I <u>used to</u> love visiting my grandmother

Would for hypothetical, imagined and conditional situations:

Example	Meaning
It **would be** nice to travel to France	*But we're travelling to France at the moment so the statement is hypothetical although it's also a future possibility*
If I *had* a million pounds, I **would buy** a big house	*I don't have a million pound so I'm talking about something imaginary.*
If we *had worked* harder we **would have finished** by now	*But we didn't work harder so we haven't finished so the sentence is hypothetical*

Would to introduce opinions and advice:

Example	Meaning

I **would say** that the red colour is better	*A polite way to give an opinion*
I **would think** that it's better to try	*A polite way way to provide an opinion if you're not sure*
You **would imagine** it's difficult but it's not	*A polite way to suggest what your opinion might be and that it's possibly wrong*
I **wouldn't say** that if I were you	*I **advise you** not to say that / **In my opinion** you shouldn't say that*
I **would suggest** you ask for a refund	*In my opinion / it's my advise that you ask for a refund*

Would to talk about what is wanted, desired or willingness:

Example	Meaning
I **would stay** longer but I have to catch a bus	*I **want** / I **am willing** to stay longer but I have to catch a bus* *(would as a hypothetical future)*
She wouldn't lend me her umbrella so I got wet	*She **didn't want** / **wasn't willing** to lend me her umbrella* *(would as the past tense of will)*
I **would love** some coffee	*I politely **want** / **desire** some coffee* *(using love makes the desire stronger than like)*
I **would like** to go home now	*I **want** to go home now*
Would you like to go home now?	*Do you want to go home now?*
I wish **he would go** away	*I **want** him to go away (he hasn't)* *(would as an unreal past with wish)*
I wish **it would rain**	*I **desire** rain (it's not raining)* *(would as an unreal past with wish)*

I would like, would you like? I would love etc. are common expressions to politely say what you want.

Expressions with *wish* always use the unreal past tense to indicate that you're talking about something that is not real.

For example:

- *I <u>wish</u> I <u>had</u> a million pounds (but I don't have a million pounds so it's not real, it's just a wish).*

Therefore *would* is commonly used with wish as the past (unreal) tense of will.

Would for requests:

Example	Meaning
Would you open the window?	*I politely ask you to open the window*
Would you pass me the book please?	*I politely ask you to pass me the book.*

NOTE: Will is also grammatically correct for requests and can be used in some very informal situations. However, using preterite (past) forms is considered more polite in English so 'would' is preferred in most situations. Non-native speakers are strongly advised to use 'would' for all requests in all situations.

Would to introduce preferences:

Example	Meaning
I would prefer to go to France instead of Spain	*I politely say that I'd prefer to go to France*
I would rather not speak about it	*I politely say that I prefer not to speak about it*

NOTE: *'I would prefer...' and 'I would rather...' are very common expressions used to introduce a preference. They have a near identical meaning and are usually contracted in informal English - 'I'd prefer... I'd rather...'*

It's not grammatically necessary to use would with prefer but we use it to give a conditional feeling to the statement which makes it softer.

Would to introduce a doubt:

Example	Meaning
She would appear to be unhappy	*She seems to be unhappy (and I'm not entirely sure why)*
The **shop would appear** to be closed	*The shop seems to be closed (and I'm surprised or not sure why)*

She appears to be unhappy is also a valid expression but the insertion of *would* indicates that there is an uncertainty in the situation.

Would for disapproval:

Example	Meaning
He would say that, *wouldn't he*?	*I expected him to say that and I disapprove or don't believe him*
She thinks she did well. *She would, wouldn't she?*	*I disapprove of her thinking that she did well*

NOTE: When using would to express our disapproval we generally add a tag question to emphasise the disapproval, as shown in the table above.

Would + that for regret:

Example	Meaning
Would that it were (true)	*I wish it were true*
Would that he had lived to see this	*I wish he had lived to see this*

NOTE: *This construction is unlikely to be heard often in everyday speech as it is very formal and more often used in poetic or literary writing.*

7.6.3 USED TO

The semi-modal verb *'used to'* expresses past habitual actions that are no longer happening. It is followed by an infinitive main verb.

It has a near identical meaning to *would* where *would* is used to express past habitual actions. However, unlike *would* as a past habit, *used to* may also be used with non-stative main verbs.

- I *used to like* ice cream but now I don't

The modal verb use of *used to* should not be confused with the adjective *used to* which means *familiar with*. The adjective use of *used to* is easily identified as it never followed by an infinitive main verb but by a noun, pronoun or the gerund form of a main verb. For example:

- *I am **used to her** ways* or *I am **used to waiting** a long time (Adjectives)*
- *When I was young I **used to play** football in the park (semi-modal)*

The main verb *used,* meaning employed, may also appear with a *to-infinitive*, for example;

- *Bricks are **used to** build houses.*

The context makes it obvious that we are talking about *used* as a main verb and not *used to* as a semi-modal verb describing past habits.

In speech we show the difference by using a different sound for the endings. For *used to* as a semi-modal verb we pronounce it as *use<u>t</u> to* with a 't' sound for the 'd'. For *used* as a past of the main verb *use* we pronounce the final 'd' as a 'd' as in *bricks are use<u>d</u> to build houses.*

I <u>used to</u> play football when I was younger (I regularly played football when I was younger)

- Questions with used to

Unlike pure modal verbs, *used to* uses the auxiliary verb *do* to form questions. Since the auxiliary verb *do* forms the past tense in questions, *used to* reverts to the present tense form *use to.*

- **Did you use to play** football when you were younger?

It is possible grammatically to invert *used* and the *subject* to form questions as in *used you to play football?* This sounds very old fashioned and is no longer used by native speakers. It may be found in antique literature.

- Negatives with used to

The negative is formed by using the auxiliary verb do. As do forms the past tense, *used to* reverts to the present tense form.
For example:

- *He **didn't use to** live here.*

The negative could be formed by reversing the *subject* and *used* but this is now very rare and is usually found only in literature written many years ago.

UNIT 8: MODALITIES

8.1. ABILITY

Ability is expressed by using the modal verbs *can* and *could* and the semi-modal **to be able to.**

8.1.1 Present ability: can and is/are able to

Present ability	Meaning
I *can* swim very well	*I have the ability to swim very well*
I'm *able to* swim very well	*I have the ability to swim very well*
I *can't* play guitar	*I don't have the ability to play guitar*
I'm *not able* to play guitar	*I don't have the ability to play guitar*

Can and *is/are able to* are used interchangeably in the present tense with very little difference in meaning.

8.1.2 Past ability: could and was/were not able to:

Past ability	Meaning
When I was young, I *could* swim very well	*When I was young, I had the ability to swim very well*
They *were able to* swim very well	*They had the ability to swim very well*
They *were not able* to play guitar	*They didn't have the ability to play guitar*
They *couldn't* play guitar	*They didn't have the ability to play guitar*

Could and *was/were able to* are used interchangeably in the past tense with little difference in meaning.

Because *can* and *could* are defective, we use the semi-modal *to be able to* to form all other tenses.

8.1.3 Other abilities: be able to

Future ability	Meaning
I **will be able to** get there by next weekend	*I have the ability to get there by next weekend*
I **won't be able to** get there until the weekend	*I won't have the ability to get there until the weekend (when I will have the ability)*

Conditional ability	Meaning
I **would be able to** come if I had a car	I would have the ability to come if I owned a car. (But I don't)

Present perfect ability	Meaning
I **haven't been able to** repair your radio yet	*I haven't had the ability to repair your radio yet*

Subjunctive ability	Meaning
I demand that he **be able to** speak	*I demand that he is given the ability to speak (but I know it's not in my power so it may not happen)*

8.2 ADVICE, SUGGESTIONS & RECOMMENDATIONS

We use *should, ought to* and *had better* to give advice, suggestions and recommendations.

Should and *ought to* are very similar and often used interchangeably but, for many native speakers, *should* has a softer tone between the two option whereas *ought to* can be considered more objective.

Had better often provides a much stronger tone with the implication of something negative happening if the advice/suggestion/recommendation is not followed.

1. We **should** go home – *My advice/recommendation is that we go home*

2. We **ought to** go home – *My advice/recommendation is that we go home (there's a good reason for this advice, such as it's late, you're drunk etc.)*

3. We **had better** go home – *My advice/recommendation is that we go home (because if we don't there's going to be trouble or I won't be able to get up for work etc.)*

In practice, the differences shown above are very slight. Many native speakers often use *should* and *ought to* based on the preference of the speaker for one form or the other and to avoid repetition.

- We **should** go home but we **ought to** thank our hosts first – *I* **suggest** *we go home but I* **suggest** *we thank our hosts first*
- We **should/ought to** go home but we**'d better** thank our hosts first – *I* **suggest** *we go home but I* **suggest** *we thank our hosts first (otherwise they may think we are rude)*

8.2.1 Advice and recommendations given by outside authorities

Should is usually used when talking about the advice/recommendations of a third party authority. For example:

- Drivers **should** be more careful in icy conditions – *the advice is being given by the government or motorist organisations not the person speaking.*
- Drivers **ought to** be more careful in icy conditions – *a statement of advice given by the speaker*

8.2.2 Questions

Should is more usual than *ought to* in questions:

- Who *should* I ask?
- *Should* I bring sandwiches?

Using *ought to* in questions is not wrong but sounds rather formal and old-fashioned.

8.2.3 Criticism about a past action

When we express criticism or regret about a past action we can use *should* and *shouldn't* and sometimes, *ought to*, with the past perfect.

Example	Meaning
We **should/ought to go** and see the new Star Wars film	*My advice/recommendation is to go and see the new Star Wars film*
We **should/ought to have gone** to see the new Star Wars film, I heard it was very good	*I regret not going to the new Star Wars film*
You failed your driving test, you **should/ought to have practised** more	*I am criticising you for not practising more*
You **should/ought to practise** if you want to pass your driving test	*I recommend/advise that you practice*
You have a headache? You **shouldn't have drunk** so much wine	*I am criticising you for drinking too much win*

8.3 POSSIBILITY

Different levels of possibility are expressed using the modal verbs *can, could, may, might* and *should.*

8.3.1 Different possibilities

Typically *might* is considered more informal than *may* which is used for more formal situations or in formal descriptions about possibility.

Could indicates a stronger possibility with the implication of ability.

Can is used to indicate that something is *generally* possible.

Should expresses a possibility based on deduction or evidence.

Example	Meaning
I **might** go to the party later	It's possible I'll go to the party later
The government **may** change the law	It's possible that the government will change the law
The government **could** change the law	The government has the ability to change the law but it's not certain they will
It **can** rain a lot in winter	It's very possible that it will rain in winter as it generally rains a lot at that time
We're the better team so we **should** win	It's probable that we'll win as the deduction is that we're the better team
I've been working on this for a week so I **should** be finished soon	It's very likely that I'll be finished soon based on the evidence that I've been working for a week on it

8.3.2 Present possibilities

Present possibility is usually expressed using *may, might* or *could*, often using the gerund form of the verb to show that something is happening as we speak.

Native speakers generally use may for the least possible situation, might for the next level of possibility and could for the most possible level.

Example	Meaning
I think he **may/might/could be coming now**	I think it's possible he's coming now
I'm not sure where she is. She **may/might/could be shopping**	It's possible she's shopping
She **may/might/could have** a cold	It's possible she has a cold

8.3.3 Future possibilities

We often use *may, might, should* and *could* to express different degrees of future possibility.

Could indicates a stronger possibility in some situations but also has the implication of *ability* associated with the possibility so generally we will often use *may* or *might to ensure the listener understands we are talking about possibility.*

Example	Meaning
I **may/might** go to the party later	*There's a possibility I will go to the party later*
I **could** go to the party later	*I have the ability to go to the party but it's possible it won't happen*
I **might** be taking driving lessons next year	*It's possible I'll be taking driving lessons next year*
I **should** be taking driving lessons next year	It's very possible that I'll take driving lessons next year

8.3.4 Past possibilities

When we talk about past possibility we use: *might / may / could + have + past participle.* The same levels of possibility are used for each modal verb as for present and future, may being the least possible and could the most.

Example	Meaning
They **may/might not have left** yet	*It's possible that they haven't left yet*
I don't know where he is, he **might have gone** shopping	*It's possible he's gone shopping*
It **could have happened** that way	*It's possible it happened that way*

8.3.5 Possibility in Questions

Could is often used is questions about possibility when some ability is implied in the possibility. *Might* is sometimes used but sounds too formal for most situations. *May* is never used in questions about possibility as may expresses hope when the subject and verb is reversed.

For example:

Example	Meaning
Could they really win?	*Is it possible they have the ability to win?*
Might they win?	*Is it possible that they will win? (Very formal, more common is **are they likely to win**)*
May they win.	*This is not a question but a formal statement of hope that they win*

NOTE: *When used in this sense, 'should' and 'ought to' almost always occur with verbs and expressions which express a positive meaning:*

- *My team should/ought to win the match – I expect my team to win the match*
- **NOT** *my team* ~~should/ought to~~ *lose – (this means that my team deserves to lose)*

8.4 PROBABILITY, DEDUCTION & CERTAINTY

Must, have to, have got to, should, ought to, will, can't and *couldn't* are the modal verbs used to express deduction and certainty. The certainty expressed by the modal verbs is the result of a deduction which is not always stated.

Should and *ought to* are used to indicate an assumption expressing that something is probable based on past experience or evidence.

When talking about probability, there is little or no difference between *should* and *ought to*.

Must and *have (got)* to are used for a near certainty but care should be taken as they also express obligation and there is a risk of ambiguity. Therefore the context should be made clear. Stress is often used to provide the meaning.

Will and *won't* also express a very strong probability or a near certainty. They are used when we are very sure about something

Can't is used for the negative form of *must* when used for deduction. *Must not* or *mustn't* can only be used as an instruction or obligation.

8.4.1 Present probabilities, deductions and certainties

Example	Meaning
We **should/ought to** finish by 6 o'clock	*We expect to finish/assume we will finish by 6 o'clock (because we have the experience to know this)*
The parcel **should/ought to** arrive by Wednesday	*I expect it to arrive/assume it will arrive by Wednesday (because I know how long parcels usually take to arrive)*
You **must** be cold	*My deduction is that you're cold (I can see that you're shivering and I know it's below freezing outside)*
There **has to/must** be a mistake	*I am certain/my deduction is that there's a mistake*
They**'ve got to/must** be your	*I am certain they are yours / my deduction is that they are yours (because I know they aren't mine)*
It **can't** be Jane upstairs, she's not here	*My deduction is that it's not Jane upstairs as I know she's not here*
John **will** be studying in his bedroom	*I am certain that John is studying in his bedroom right now (because I know he does that every night)*
John **must** be studying in his bedroom	*I have deduced that John is studying in his bedroom (as he's not here studying)*
John **should** be studying in his bedroom	*I expect that John is studying in his bedroom (but he might not be)*

NOTE: *test books and* course *materials often teach that we use* **will** *rather than* **must** *when our deduction is based on evidence such as our knowledge of typical or repeated behaviour. In everyday English,* **will** *and* **must** *are often used interchangeably by native speakers.*

8.4.2 Past probabilities, deductions and certainties

Had to and *should/ought to, must, will* + have + past participle can be used to talk about something that probably happened in the past.

Example	Meaning
It **had to** be John who took them	*I have deduced/almost certain that John took them (because I know he as there and he's untrustworthy)*
He **should/ought to have arrived** by now	*I expect that he arrived earlier and is no there*
The chocolate isn't there, someone **must've eaten** it	*I deduce that someone has eaten it (because it's gone and I now I didn't eat it)*
I expected John to be home by now. His train **must have been** delayed	*I have deduced that the reason for John's lateness is that his train was delayed*
They **will have arrived** by now	*I'm certain they have arrived and are there (because they told me when they were arriving)*
They **must have arrived** by now	*I deduce that they have arrived and are there (because I expected it.)*

NOTE: *Have got to* is used for present deductions only – **NOT** It *had ~~got~~ to* be John who took it.

8.4.3 Future probabilities, deductions and certainties

Will is used to talk about something that is almost certainly true in the near future because you have some knowledge or evidence.

Must is also used for future deduction but expresses expectation or hope rather than evidence.

Should / ought to is used when the future deduction is less certain.

Example	Meaning
Can you answer the phone? That'**ll** be my mother calling	*I'm certain that's my mother calling (she always calls a this time)*
Can you answer the phone? It **should** be my mother	*I expect it will be my mother (but it might not be)*
Can you answer the phone? That **must** be my mother	*I deduce that is my mother calling (as she always calls at this time)*

8.5 POLITE REQUESTS

Modal verbs are used in requests to show politeness. Polite requests are formed using can, could, will and would. *May* is also used for formal polite requests when using 1st person pronoun.

Although requests can be formed using *can* and *will*, the preterite forms are preferred as they provide the remoteness necessary to provide politeness. Using the preterite forms *could or would* means the request is not an expectation. This therefore shows that you're not assuming the person you are asking is going to grant your request and in this way it conveys politeness.

For example:

- **Pass me the phone.** *Using the imperative form of a main verb means that the request is an instruction rather than a request. Note the lack of a question mark. The listener may become offended at the directness of this request.*

- **Can (or will) you pass me the phone?** *Often used for requests when politeness is not necessary, for example between close friends or work colleagues. However Native speakers will often try to avoid this constructions for <u>polite</u> requests for two reasons. Firstly although softer than using the imperative of a main verb, it still sounds like an instruction rather than a request. Secondly the meaning can be ambiguous. Using can also means that you are asking if the listener has the ability to pass the phone? Will is often preferred for this reason.*

- **Could (or would) you pass me the phone?** *The preterite forms give a lack of expectation and hence politeness. If you're unsure of the context of your request, you should always use could or would to form a polite request.*

- ***May I*** borrow your phone? *- A formal polite request to borrow the phone*

- ***May we*** come in? *- A formal polite request to enter.*

8.6 GIVING PERMISSION

Can, could and *may* are used to express the idea of giving permission to do something or to talk generally about permission.

May is often used to talk about permission in formal contexts. *Might* is occasionally used for permission but is generally avoided as it can sound too formal.

Example	Meaning
You *can* borrow my phone	*You have permission to borrow my phone*
You *may* borrow my phone	*You have permission to borrow my phone (formal)*
You *can't* borrow my phone	*You don't have permission to borrow my phone*
You *may not* borrow my phone	*You don't have permission to borrow my phone (formal)*
We *couldn't* have a cat in our flat	*We were not able to have a cat in our flat*

NOTE: *Remember, the preterite of might is not the past tense of may. Therefore, we might not have a cat in our flat means that there's a possibility that we don't have a cat and is not about permission or a past.*

8.7 INTENTIONS, PROMISES & WILLINGNESS

Will, shall and *would* are used to state an intention or willingness to do something or to promise to do something.

Example	Meaning
I'*ll* repair this tomorrow	*I intend/promise to repair this tomorrow (will or shall – future)*
We'*ll* look at this later	*We promise to look at this later (will or shall – future)*
I *won't/shan't* touch it	*I promise not to touch it (future)*
Do you think she *will* take them?	*Do you think she is willing to take them?*

	(future)
They **won't** be coming	*They have no intention of coming (future)*
I did try to persuade her, but she **wouldn't** come	*She wasn't willing to come (past)*
If I asked nicely, do you think she **would** come?	*Do you think she is willing to come if I were to ask her? (2nd conditional)*

8.8 OBLIGATION, NECESSITY & PROHIBITION

Must, have to and *have got to* are all used to express obligation and necessity. *Must* generally expresses the obligation of the speaker and *have (got) to* the obligation of *someone* or *something* who is not the speaker *Need to* is used to express necessity.

Example	Meaning
Applicants **must** answer al the questions	*Applicants are obliged to answer all the questions. The obligation is set by the speaker or writer*
Applicants **have (got) to** answer all the questions	*Applicants are obliged to answer all the questions. The obligation is not set by the speaker/writer but by someone or something else*
Applicants **need to** answer all the questions	*It's necessary that the applicants answer all the questions*

8.8.1 Questions

The question forms of *have to* and *must* ask whether you are obliged to do something. They follow the same implication as the present forms where *must* implies that the listener is setting the obligation and have to implies an external person or body is setting the obligation.

Example	Meaning
Do I have to answer all the questions?	*Am I obliged to answer all the questions?*
Must I answer all the questions	*Am I obliged to answer all the questions?*
Need I answer all the questions	*Is it necessary for me to answer all the questions?*

NOTE: *Have (got) to is more common than must when asking questions about whether something is an obligation. Must in questions sounds rather formal and old-fashioned for many native speakers.*

8.8.2 Negatives

Don't have to, haven't got to, needn't/need not and don't need to all express a lack of obligation, necessity or prohibition. *Must not / mustn't* is used to express prohibition, for example:

You must not smoke

Examples:

Example	Meaning
Applicants **must not** call the office	*Applicants are prohibited from calling the office*
Applicants **don't have to** call the office	*It's not necessary / there's no obligation for applicants to call the office*
Applicants **haven't got to** call the office	*It's not necessary / there's no obligation for applicants to call the office (informal)*
Applicants **don't need to / needn't** call the office	*It's not necessary for applicants to call the office*

8.8.3 Other obligations

Example	Meaning
I **will have to** work hard (future)	*I will be obliged to work harder*
I **had to** work harder (past)	*I was obliged to work harder (but now I'm not)*
I **have had to** work harder (perfect)	*I was obliged to work harder (and I am still working harder)*

I **did have to** work harder   I was obliged to work harder (until something
(past perfect)   else happened)

8.9 HABITS

Will, *would* and *used to* are the modals used to describe habits, repeated actions or characteristic behaviours. *Will* is used for habits, actions or behaviour in the present or future and *would* and *used to* for habits, actions or behaviours in the past.

I used to be a

runner when I was younger

The *present simple* or *past simple* tenses, often with an *adverb of frequency,* is a common way to speak or write about habits.

For example:

- We **go** to the park every Saturday (present habit)
- We **went** to the park every Saturday (past habit)

However, we regularly use modals to make it clear that you are speaking about a *regular* habit.

8.9.1 Present habits

Example	Meaning
I **will** usually go to a football match on Saturdays	*It's normal behaviour for me to go to a football match on Saturdays*
My father **will** always complain about politicians	*It's normal behaviour for my father to regularly complain about politicians*

Will also expresses obstinate or annoying regular behaviours or habits. The context gives the meaning.

Example	Meaning
She **will** insist on arriving late	*She always arrives late and it's annoying*
If you **will** keep ignoring him then he's not going to help you	*If you are obstinate and keep ignoring him then he's not going to help you*

8.9.2 Past habits

Used to and *would* are used for describing past habits and behaviours. They are, however, not always interchangeable.

We _don't_ use *would* with *stative verbs*. Stative verbs describe things that are not actions. For example, the verbs believe, think and understand are stative.

Example	Meaning
When I was a child, my father **would** read to me at night	*My father regularly read to me (there may be some nostalgia attached)*
When I was a child my father **read** to me every night	*My father regularly read to me*
When I was a child my father **used to** read to me every night	*My father regularly read to me*

Whenever the sentence contains a stative verb we must use *used to* (or *past simple + adverb of frequency*) to speak about past habits:

Example	Meaning
We **used to live** in Spain but we moved to London last year	*We lived in Spain in the past*
We **lived** in Spain but we moved to London last year	*We lived in Spain in the past*
We ~~would~~ **live** in Spain but we moved to London last year **X**	*Live is a stative verb so we can't use would*

NOTE: *Would + stative verb has a <u>conditional</u> or <u>hypothetical</u> meaning and therefore cannot be a past habit. For example:*

I would live in Spain if I spoke Spanish (but I don't)

NOTE: *When we are talking or writing about past habits, behaviours and repeated actions we use a mix of would, used to and past simple where appropriate.*
This is to avoid repetition and to make things sound more interesting.

8.10 HYPOTHETICALS & CONDITIONALS

Preterite modal verbs perform a function known as modal remoteness. This allows us to express hypothetical and conditional situations and actions.

Imagine I won the lottery, I could buy a new car.

8.10.1 CONDITIONAL SITUATIONS

The conditional allows us to talk about a situation and a future action that is conditional. The resultant action is therefore hypothetical or imaginary.

The example '*Imagine I won the lottery, I could buy a new car*' above is a 2nd conditional which asks the listener or reader to imagine a future where I win the lottery. The first part of the clause contains the verb in a past tense, known as an unreal past (*won* in the example above) to provide remoteness and to therefore show the expression is not a fact.

Preterite modal verbs are used in all 2nd and 3rd conditional constructions to show present, future or past hypothetical and conditional situations.

Conditional sentences are an entire grammar topic in their own right so are outside the scope of this book but here are some examples:

Example	Meaning
If you *went* to London, you *might* see the Prime Minister of the UK (2nd conditional)	If you go to London in the future, maybe you will see the Prime Minister of the UK
Suppose I *had* a better job, I *would* be much happier (2nd conditional)	I don't have a better job and I'm not happy, I'm just imagining something
If you *had studied* more, you *would have passed* your exams (3rd conditional)	But you didn't study more and you didn't pass so it's a past condition that didn't happen

Preterite modal verbs are used in a wide range of sentences to show conditional meanings by using the remoteness.

For example:

- Why don't you ask her? I'm sure she *would* help you.

In this example, using the preterite modal *would* provides the suggestion that you need to ask her to get her help but that she won't help you if you don't ask (the condition). If you used *she will help you* you are stating that she's ready and waiting to help you, which she hasn't as you haven't asked her yet.

8.10.2 IMAGINARY SITUATIONS

Sentences using the words *wish* or *if only* introduce imaginary situations. The verb used with these sentences will be an unreal past (or a past subjunctive) to indicate the remoteness from a real situation. When a modal verb is required it will always therefore be the preterite form to indicate a counter factual condition.

Examples	Meaning
I **wish** you **would** visit me more often	I don't know if you will visit me more often so the situation I want is hypothetical
If only I **could** earn more money	I can't earn more money so the situation I'm describing is imaginary

UNIT 9: PRONUNCIATION & STRESS

9.1 PRONUNCIATION & STRESS FOR MEANING

Pronunciation and stress is an area that is often neglected when looking at the meanings of modals in spoken English. Learning modal grammar, uses and definitions is of course fundamental but not always sufficient when using spoken English with native speakers.

The true meaning of what is being said can be missed or misunderstood without understanding why they are using particular pronunciations and stresses. In many cases the pronunciation of modal verbs is so weak it can be missed by non-native speakers unused to how they are said in real life.

Different meanings can be given to sentences containing modal verbs and semi-modals by using of different pronunciations and stresses.

English speakers pronounce modal verbs in one of two different ways depending on the meaning they wish to impart; **strong pronunciation** or **weak pronunciation**.

9.2 STRONG PRONUNCIATION

The modal verb is pronounced clearly and strongly when you want to ask questions or provide emphasis. It is also used is answers to questions when you don't want to repeat the main verb.

For example:

- Person 1: **Can** *you speak French?*
- Person 2: *Yes. I* **can.**

9.3 WEAK PRONUNCIATION

The modal verb is pronounced softly and quickly – the vowel and sometimes the final consonant is reduced or even missed out entirely. This is the most common form of modal verb pronunciation used by native speakers.

For example:

- *I* **c'n** *(can) see the mountains from my room*
- *you* **c'd** *(could) try later or you* **c'** *try later*
- *we* **sh'd** *(should) go to the play or we* **sh'** *go to the play*

9.4 PRONUNCIATION OF MODALS WITH TO

In most cases, the **to** that follows a modal is pronounced with a shortened **e** sound. This is common with how **to** is often pronounced in general English.

The shortened **e** sound is known as the *schwa* and is shown as a ə symbol in grammar books.

For example:

- *We ought tə leave soon.*

- *You have tə take the second turning on the left.*

- *We need tə **leave.***

9.5 STRESS

Certain words in spoken modal sentences are stressed to make the meaning clear. Often the stress is combined with strong or weak pronunciation or contractions.

For example:

- We **<u>may</u>** go next week – The stress on may indicates the possibility of going next week.

- *We may go <u>next</u> week* – The stress on *next* indicates that it's possible we'll go next week rather than this week

- *She <u>**will**</u> do that* – The stress on the strong form of *will* indicates that I'm saying she has an annoying habit and that she continually does it.

- *She'll do that* – The contraction and weak form of *will* with no stress indicates that I promise she will do something (in the future)

THE END

Copyright © Alexander Markham 2023

About the author

Alexander Markham is a CELTA tutor from London. He has worked in a variety of business roles around the world using his second and third languages before becoming a qualified English tutor.

Alwexander holds the Cambridge University approved CELTA teaching qualification as well as a Master's degree in Business and Modern Languages qualifications in Spanish and French.

As a tutor, Alex works with professional and business students from around the world, helping them to improve their English at advanced level and for Cambridge exams such as IELTS, CAE and CPE.

Alex writes free articles on aspects of advanced-level English. You can connect with him at:

Website: www.theenglishbureau.com
Facebook: https://www.facebook.com/theenglishbureau/
Pinterest: https://www.pinterest.co.uk/theenglishburea/

Learn how to use modal verbs, one of the most important areas of English grammar. You will find out the meanings and correct contexts for every modal and semi-modal verb and how to use alternative or substitute constructions when necessary. The book covers not only each meaning of every modal and semi-modal verb but also the relationships between them, the characteristics and rules and the often neglected area of pronunciations and stresses used by native speakers. Soft and weak pronunciations in spoken English, for example, impart different meanings, an area rearely covered in standard courses or grammar books. In addition Learn Real English Modal Verbs covers real English uses of modals, showing you the way that native speakers really use modals which isn't always how grammar books and English courses teach.

A FREE BONUS Modal Verb Pronunciation Guide with associated 53 online audio recordings is available to download with every purchase of this book. Learn how to identify and understand modal verbs in real spoken English with this free supplement. Suitable for learners of English as a Second Language, English tutors and those wanting to brush up on the grammar of Modal Auxiliary Verbs.

* 9 7 9 8 3 7 5 5 3 3 2 2 3 *